THE LOVELY SIGHT OF ITHACA

THE LOVELY SIGHT OF ITHACA

A Modest Volume of Poetry in Traditional Forms

MICHAEL JAMIESON WILLIAMS

RESOURCE *Publications* • Eugene, Oregon

THE LOVELY SIGHT OF ITHACA
A Modest Volume of Poetry in Traditional Forms

Copyright © 2022 Michael Jamieson Williams. All rights reserved. Except for brief quotations in critical publications or reviews, no part of this book may be reproduced in any manner without prior written permission from the publisher. Write: Permissions, Wipf and Stock Publishers, 199 W. 8th Ave., Suite 3, Eugene, OR 97401.

Resource Publications
An Imprint of Wipf and Stock Publishers
199 W. 8th Ave., Suite 3
Eugene, OR 97401

www.wipfandstock.com

PAPERBACK ISBN: 978-1-6667-5762-0
HARDCOVER ISBN: 978-1-6667-5763-7
EBOOK ISBN: 978-1-6667-5764-4

DECEMBER 7, 2022 12:24 PM

Unless otherwise indicated, all Scripture quotations are from the *Douay-Rheims* translation of the Holy Bible.

This book is dedicated to my best friends
KATHERINE OSBORNE-HIGHTOWER
and
MARTIN GLAVES

CONTENTS

Author's Note | xi
Preface | xiii
The Glacier | 1
Conversion I | 2
Serenity Invincible | 3
Chronic | 4
10/26/21—5:30 AM | 7
Consider the Lupines | 8
Sunset's Epilogue | 10
The Roads Too Much Taken | 14
On Reading Thomas Kearney's Memoir of His Travels Through the New World | 15
"The Haze on the Horizon" | 17
Paradox | 18
Cinquains | 20
First Snowfall | 21
To Some Eastward Hills | 23
"He Was a Demigod of Youth's Ideal" | 24
Single Life Blues | 27
To a Certain Kitty | 29
Portrait of a Crisis | 30

Avian Gospel | 31
"All Sorrowful Am I and All Too Stolid" | 32
Sonnets For Katherine | 33
Amazing, Sweet | 37
Priorities | 38
Meteor Conflict | 40
kyrie eleison | 41
"I Was the Leaf You Trod Upon" | 42
Rentboy Blues | 43
St. Thomas on Mission | 45
For The Old Man in His Twilight | 46
A Posthumous Competition | 47
"False Romances Swarm Me Like Locusts a Field" | 50
"Ain't Easy to Be Catholic and Gay" | 52
The Raven's Soliloquy | 53
"My Life is Constant Autumn" | 55
Europe is the Less | 57
For Tanner | 59
The Last Poem | 60
"Impotence Raves at a Deaf Universe" | 62
The Cautionary Tale of Pugnacious Peter | 63
Doggerel by a Homebody | 66
Doggerel on Beatitude | 68
"What is it 'Bout a Summer Night" | 69
Who Would Fardels Bear? | 71
The Pomegranate Tree | 72
Between Insanity and Doubt | 73
Self-Rebuke | 74
The Search for Euterpe | 75

"I Would Have Handled Them with Greater Care" | 76

Astronomical Doggerel | 77

"Obscured Azure: The Heavens' Airy Fountains" | 78

"Recipient of Mustard Seed" | 79

Conversion II | 80

Doggerel by an Irresolute Fellow | 81

Decline and Fall | 82

Ballad of Madness | 83

"Exotical Neurology" | 85

Reason in the Face of Madness | 87

Incremental Immutability | 89

Writer's Block | 91

AUTHOR'S NOTE

"Writer's Block" first appeared in the November/December 2019 issue of *The Saint Austen Review*; "Conversion" and "The Last Poem" appeared in the January/February 2021 issue, and "Serenity Invincible" appeared in the November/December 2021 of the same publication.

The following poems first appeared in *The New English Review*: "Recipient of Mustard Seed" and "Self-Rebuke" in October 2020; "What Is It 'Bout A Summer Night" and "Meteor Conflict" (under the title "Pretty Follies, II") in November 2020; "Single Life Blues" and "Chronic" in December 2020; "Conversion II" and "kyrie eleison" in February 2022.

"On Reading Thomas Kearney's Memoir of His Travels Through the New World," first appeared in *White Rose Magazine* in December 2021.

PREFACE

A KIND FRIEND ONCE told me that I am "a seriously autobiographical poet." Perhaps, but I live and write under the stricture that no autobiography of mine is worth the ink unless it corresponds in some way to the experience and sentiments of others. One of these universal themes is that of the inner conflict between two contradictory principles, both of which are true, but which do violence to each other when contact is made within a single human mind, resulting in recurrent and frenzied stalemates. Another is the longing for peace and reconciliation within the soul, when all discordant precepts are harmonized, and the soul's sight can then be firmly fixed on the goal or goals of one's own spiritual or existential life. The yearning for this kind of serenity is, in my opinion, akin to the yearning for one's soulmate (whether one has yet met them), or for the yearning of a Promised Land, or greater still, the yearning to go home.

Imagine the joy of Moses on the mountaintop, beholding the land meant for the Children of Israel, and the sorrow he must have felt knowing he would never cross over Jordan in this life. Imagine the excitement of Odysseus being just off the shore of his island home only, moments later, to be blown off-course and then condemned to wander the earth for an additional decade, enduring every manner of hardship along the way. How indomitable was the nostalgia that moved him on his journey, and how bitter until he realized his destination. Hence the title of this present volume.

Another friend described my poetry as "combining equal parts whimsy and anguish." I suppose that's fair; we live in a vale of tears after all, and there's no use sugar-coating reality with

Preface

empty optimism. Then again, life in this world is also a minefield of laughter. The refulgence of joy and treasury of glamor in human existence is sometimes so overpowering and exciting that I crave a sedative. Nor can we neglect—if we are bold enough to assert it—the hope of eternity, the merits of which are scattered throughout our mortal duration like dandelion seeds in summer. Best to experience, endure, and express both principles without commingling or diluting either.

One theme that I know also to be prevalent in my work is that of solitude, whether to wallow in or escape from it. I also know that the earth teems with folks like me: melancholic, lonely, out-of-the-swim, always hearing the marching band playing in another street. One might think one is an island entire of itself, but beneath the profound ocean of isolation lies the floor and bedrock of our common humanity, as well as the adamantine attachments to our Creator. As the Psalmist says, "Deep calleth unto deep."

-M.J.W.
Anchorage, Alaska
July 2022

THE GLACIER

From the icy shroud of my mother the cloud
Falls the host of her crystalline tears—
Like a widow friendless, her sorrow is endless;
She weeps for a thousand years.
Her ancient woe engenders the snow;
Like a deluge it blankets the earth.
And as the centuries pass, it hardens *en masse*
Into adamant, giving me birth.

I broaden the alleys of canyons and valleys
And quarry the depths of fjords,
And the mountains efface with relentless grace
For the eons that Nature affords.
For as the earth turns like unfinished urns
Of clay on the Potter's wheel,
Grinding summits to sands, I'm the Potter's hands
As He molds and shapes and feels.

I march to the tune that moves the moon
And tread with the pace of the stars.
(To the restive and veering eye appearing
Constant, yet moving we are.)
With eternal pride, I silently glide
In an infinitesimal shiver;
With invincible force, I follow my course
To my end: the source of a river.

CONVERSION I

   The night was fertile for awakening
And I, compliant to complacency,
   Was unsuspecting of the quickening
That loomed with gathering adjacency.
   Gestating all my life, now sudden seizes
My unsuspecting self, great labor pain;
   Initiated by the chilly breezes
Of fear (first faint, then fierce) which did maintain
   A greatly unwelcome reality:
I was the patient of an operation
   Of grace—receiver of sodality.
I broke, then breathed the words of resignation
    And trudged to hospital through snow and shivered,
    Until the church door reached and was delivered.

SERENITY INVINCIBLE

Cook Inlet, at the end of day, in summer:
  Hosts of remote slate-blue or snow-draped peaks
Drenched in the sherbet hues of sunset. Gold,
        Then orange, and then pink.

Declining Sol's inferno torches clouds
  Low-lying in the distance, swelled with rain,
Creating nebulae that float above
        Stupendous, sylvan vastness.

The undulating carpet of the bay,
  Refulgent with a swathe of solar glory
And little spangles of the self-same light,
        Is respirating beauty.

This is the privilege of the pensive lad
  Alone upon the bluff (the medicine
For wistfulness and youth's febrility,
        Desire's opiate,

Breath of respite to restless novice minds,
  Reviviate of constant tedium
Which necrotizes all the glee and glamor
        Of fresh and vernal manhood):

To gaze upon God's Easel—and like nectar
  Dribbling in rivulets when flesh of fruit
Is bit and torn, to ooze with gratitude
        And humble adoration.

CHRONIC

for Lucy Fudge

Pain has an empire over me
  And spans my many members;
And as I live, there's fuel to feed
  The conquest's burning embers.

Expansive is the agony
  Whose reign is 'round me girt,
With multitudes of tribes—diverse
  Imperium of hurt.

Tyrannical of my existence,
  Enslaving concentration;
My very personality
  Is but its vassal nation:

The deluge of experience
  And life's capacity
Is dammed into a tiny stream
  Of sore mundanity.

I have naught else; this misery
  Informs my every breath:
A pregnancy perpetual,
  Delivered but by death.

And yet, more galling than my plight
  Are hearts of stone and ears
Of steel, when indeliberate swells
  A looming tide of tears.

The slam of pity's door to mute
  My song of suffering—
No likewise melody could vent
  The pungence of this sting;

The litany of judgment aired
  In stupid, cruel emissions
As if the callous fools I love
  Were suddenly physicians;

Their strange, indifferent flippancy
  Gives me no space for peace,
Nor do their torrent of demands
  And expectations cease;

I writhe in agony in bed,
  Into a ball I'm curled—
But am expected, Atlas-like,
  That I should bear their world.

Clinicians, practicing their art
  In treatment of my ill,
Regard me as a lump of ore
  That passes through a mill.

As bloodless as a statue's bronze;
  Routine as a file clerk;
Cold as a glacier to my woe.
  The doctor at her work.

Cycling sickness to a salve
  (The latter fails again);

My symptoms chase their remedy
  And I remain in pain.

Self-piteous? Indeed, I am—
  But judge me not too strict:
Were this distress and succor's dearth
  Your own self to afflict

You'd understand adversity
  And even might be crushed
Beneath that understanding's weight,
  And judgment would be hushed.

My only recourse is to faith
  So, when of tears I tire,
I place my trust in God and pray
  A rosary of fire.

10/26/21 — 5:30 AM

An early morning, chilly and banal:
The floor of heaven sponged by light pollution,
Or else obscured in swathes by clouds' dilution—
A hackneyed cigarette inhaled withal.

But shattering the shell of the mundane,
As in the swinging of a scimitar—
Bright as a firework, silent as a star,
Radiating a green and azure train

Like errant ribbons of the grand Aurora,
This emissary of the heavens came
In duel with friction to excite a flame
Wreathed in a white-hot incandescent aura.

Not some faint scratch of chalk against the board!
Instead, a vibrant, violent swipe of brush
Across a dreary canvas, all a-hush
As it cascades of burning glitter poured

Upon the sky, becoming foreign dust
Precipitately naturalized to earth.
My soul shuddered to comprehend the worth
Of such a sight that rendered me nonplussed.

Worlds of wonder escape our faint attention
As we attend the normalcy of life—
But sometimes Nature wields her awesome knife
To stab us out of lazy comprehension.

CONSIDER THE LUPINES

Lupines declare the majesty of God;
  Subtle yet striking, mild, an easy miss—
But just survey them with a conscious glimpse:
                The royal hue

That makes the eye to genuflect in awe,
  Withal the mind to whisper "Sire!" before
A tiny emperor of petals throned
                On intricate

Branches and stalks of vital, emerald tones:
  These live indeed to show the beautiful!
Alike to and exceeding trumpets blown
                Or sermons preached

They do much better than an archangel
  In sounding forth the glory of Nature's Author.
But thrones and crowns and scepters gleaming lack
                The tender touch.

Totems of earthly power show the fact
  Of might but, being lifeless, lack the blood
And breath and warmth of righteousness alone
                Which justifies

The exercise of might. These blossoms quite
  Of gentleness delineate divine
Authority by which our Cosmic Monarch
                Rules by caress.

A kindly King of vulnerability!—
  Bestrewing such bright gospels of His love,
The emissaries of His kingdom come—
                Not merely hence

But in this moment, the eternal Now.—
  This is the present and the promise both
Announcing to all those who stop and see,
                Behold and pause,

The fair ubiquity of sight and scent,
  A reign of softness, an imperium
From gardens to the pavement cracks,
  The ornament of local ambulation:
                These royal blooms.

SUNSET'S EPILOGUE

The soft blue light of vernal night
  Creeps through Venetian blinds;
A soothing balm creating calm
  In poor unquiet minds,
And such sweet peace renders release
  From misery that grinds.

All the hurry of seething worry
  That drains and stupefies
And shakes the soul out of control
  In daily, grim reprise
Is done to death by the fair breath
  Of unheard lullabies.

Daylight distracts and contracts
  The scope of consciousness
But in the gloam the soul can roam
  And ponder effortless
All things potential, existential
  Through mists of muted bliss.

And yet, despite nocturnal flight
  Of drudgery and pain
With the gladness there is sadness
  In our bed's domain;
The somber floods of pensive moods
  Still saturate the brain.

Tranquility (we can agree)
  Is not the same as "jolly"
And to suppose that in repose
  We are at rest, is folly;
The twilight time can touch the chime
  Of lucid melancholy.

Some may have lovers 'neath the covers,
  Some lie in solitude;
Some are content and some resent
  When work and play conclude;
Some sleep anon, some linger on—
  But all of us must brood.

Contemplative reflections give
  The lie to vanity;
A restive query might well harry
  Our tender sanity;
Or else we just sigh in the dust
  Of life's mundanity.

The false proportions of distortions
  Unchallenged in the day
Will with the flurry of a Fury
  Harass us when we pray
As will words flung from reckless tongue
  That we cannot unsay.

The superstitions of ambitions
  We dare to plan and cherish
Spring from the fusion of delusion
  And fervor vague and garish;
The wisest know that, like the snow,
  Most melt away and perish.

Perchance to dream, perchance to scream,
  Perchance nihility:
Unknowns to taunt and doubts to haunt
  Us with perplexity
Lest we forget the awful debt
  We owe mortality.

Did Jesus Christ engage in dice
  When coronate in brambles,
When flogged and nailed to fix the failed
  Human species' shambles,
And does He fret to place a bet
  On souls in Grace's gambles?

The chilly breeze of uncertainties
  That cause a constant shiver,
And all the flawed designs of God
  We must embrace however
Poorly the wraith of weary faith
  Can capably deliver.

Within this womb of peace and gloom
  In latter eventide
A lack of fear in musings drear
  Keeps mortals occupied;
A rarity of clarity
  That daylight can't provide.

Vigils we keep preceding sleep
  Awake, alone in bed,
Rumination's self-predations
  (The soul by selfsame fed)—

This is the chore endured before
  We imitate the dead.

THE ROADS TOO MUCH TAKEN

Two roads diverged through a wretched swamp—
Each teased with promises of false hope;
Their voices gushed with a soaring pomp,
Each wheedled me their own self to stomp;
But I, too jaded, and feeling a dope

For having baskets of years misspent
In useless hiking pursuing each
Pathway meandering as they went
Through stinking marshlands that only sent
Me dead ends, or goals out of eager reach

And, soaked in disappointment's sweat
In treading back to this same junction
To sprint the rival on a bet
And adding double the regret.
Exhausted by extreme compunction,

A cross too heavy, or liberty
Too unfulfilling for the name,
Two opposites of drudgery—
I then renounce all odyssey!
Too bored and tired to play their game,

They squawked like chickens disputing Truth;
I rolled my eyes for lack of point
Or else screamed out tirades uncouth.—
Two roads diverged to spoil my youth...
So I sat tight and smoked a joint.

ON READING THOMAS KEARNEY'S MEMOIR OF HIS TRAVELS THROUGH THE NEW WORLD

  Many, content within their cozy cells
Of soft and safe familiarity,
  Will scorn or fear the daring that compels
The youth to chase horizons, make them flee
  Until the understanding spans the whole
Continuum of all humanity.
  To tread the planet's breadth from pole to pole,
To slumber under foreign stars, and share
  Warmth with strangers through bonds of common soul
Spawns enlightenment critical and rare.

  The epic journey jointly undertaken
Toughens the sinews of a brotherhood;
  Experience's dawn shall broadly waken
A latent sympathetic hardihood.
  The road's confusion and discovery,
Its joy and danger, thrill and dullness should
  Ever embrace, like lovers' ecstasy,
To make the vistas and the grandeur sweet,
  All the mobile conviviality
Richer in slogging through the cold and heat.

  For who—but few!—have bathed in every ocean,
Or breathed the air of half the biosphere's
  Teeming diversities through global motion,
Or plunged into the reservoir of tears
  And sweat and blood exuded by the most
Of Adam's race, which evermore coheres

  Into a sea that never laps a coast?
The restless, brave, and curious alone
  Make trek to tangiate the fragile ghost
Of solidarity's prevailing groan.

  Oh, what prodigious treasure of fulfillment
Accumulated in the greed for road,
  When sandaled feet have pressed for full distillment
The liquor to the traveler bestowed!
  Oh, one like me remains ashamed to die
(Too lazy to exceed my own abode)
  And longs, one day, with fortitude to try
Some great adventure and romantic test
  Of worth in journey, and as boldly fly
As Thomas stepped the Earth in ardent quest.

"THE HAZE ON THE HORIZON"

The haze on the horizon we once treasured
Immediately in its ancient glow,
  We see through tears now from great distance measured
Which in widening makes our sorrow grow.
  But joy again may seize us in a shower
Of radiant experience and mirth—
  This too shall pass away and all its power
To gladden, as we trek the arid earth.
  Our recollections clear and dear to us
Withdrawn are from the bank of memory's saving;
  And what did lucidly appear to us
Is now the hungry void of cruel craving,
  A yearning tyranny of hollowness,
    Shreds of our lives, a wealth of nothingness.

PARADOX

Mommy had baked two plates of cookies
  And the children swarmed about her,
And plaintively they begged for some;
  Their cries grew loud and louder.

With mildness in her eyes, she said—
  Firmly, but not curt—
"Not now, my dears, you need but wait,
  For these are for dessert."

A little whimper here and there,
  But soon they were resigned
To present dearth for future joy,
  And they no longer whined.

But still, diffusing through the air
  The heady scent and sweet;
The children's patience, limned with promise
  Of such a scrumptious treat.

Now dinner-time arrived at last,
  The children were excited;
The table set, the family sat,
  And everyone delighted.

They gobbled up the roast and salad
  But yet they were not sated,
So Mommy brought the heaps of cookies
  For which the kids had waited.

And ardently they seized their prize,
  But one, the youngest, Mike,
Unnaturally desired one,
  The filthy little tyke!

He grabbed with glee a cookie, but
  Before he took a bite
His Daddy slapped it from his hands
  And snarled at him with spite:

"You wretched little shit!" he cried,
  "You make me want to spew!
If you attempt to eat dessert,
  I'll beat you black and blue!"

His siblings shook disdainful heads,
  His Mommy glared with hate;
Young Mike, confused, despondent, hurt,
  Stared at an empty plate.

CINQUAINS

My tears,
in snuffing out
the votive candle's flame,
have transubstantiated hope
to smoke.

My thoughts,
like bloodhounds, roam
in search of Heaven's scent
and finding none, descend, return
to earth.

My hands
have shrunk and dried
in atrophy like leaves
that fell last fall, forgetting how
to love.

My heart,
beneath a weight
of sacrifice, bemoans
the wood that slowly petrifies
to stone.

FIRST SNOWFALL

I wake beneath the cinder blocks
Of my self-hatred, lethargy,
And hopelessness, hating the day
But lacking the enthusiasm
To curse the sun for rising. (There's
Some whiskey left, but not enough

To make a difference.) I rise,
And with Herculean endeavor,
Plant callused feet within a garden
Of dirty socks and crumpled paper
(The drab verdure of my depression).
Scenes and jokes from the comedy

I binge-watched last night without laughing
Hum in my brain like a mild headache,
Echoing through this joyless void.
Trudging like walking wounded from
My bedroom to the living room,
I fumble, searching for the light,

The only light within my dingy,
Messy and cavernous apartment:
A pack of cigarettes, and flame.
I pull the blinds that separate
Me from my balcony, my perch
Of idle solitude and smoke—

And then, God seems to snap His fingers,
And smite me with the dazzle of
A bridal white, sepia tones,
And cloud-expatriated blue,
Which rush upon me like an army
In conquest of my field of vision,

And all my focus, taking captive.
Even the prospect of the winter's
Six-month desolation succumbs
To such a scene of purity,
The hush of fresh simplicity,
The sharp scent of frigidity.

My nerves and soul are shaken free
Of misery and self-involvement;
This gift recalls to mind the creek
That, steadily through sylvan patches,
Flows like a silver road, and as
A lover, begs to be enjoyed.

I dress and fly to the front door
That's atrophied from lack of use,
But now is healed, regaining strength;
Just a few blocks away, the stream,
The snow, the trees await to share
A gospel with an untombed corpse.

TO SOME EASTWARD HILLS

  Totems of majesty, which cast upon
A frigid city, shadows sole dispersed
  By self-same mediatrices of dawn
That filter forth the light that touched them first.
  The splendor of a bodybuilder's flex,
The proud and ermined monuments of time;
  Grandeur's temples which, viewing them, perplex
A sense of scale; souls lost in the sublime.
  The edifices of eternity,
The anchors in the swirling seas of change,
  Nature's pomp 'mid human banality,
Transporting, solemn solaces that range
  The easterly horizon, and so high
  They seem to kiss, caress the very sky.

"HE WAS A DEMIGOD OF YOUTH'S IDEAL"

He was a demigod of Youth's ideal,
A mobile sculpture, flesh and sinew cast
　In flawless, gleaming bronze that made me reel
When near to him and when desire harassed
　My mind. He was a thing Arcadian,
In fresh and gentle blitheness unsurpassed;
　The flash of glamor in quotidian
Bleak, adolescent, dingy drudgery.
　Too blessed was I at that meridian
To share an hour of his company.

The autumn air was crisp as all the trees'
Exuviation that we trod upon,
　Smoky suspicions floated through the breeze,
The sun had climbed to brilliant paragon
　Of noon in Heaven's field of cyan hue,
The cloudless kingdom's highest echelon.
　The rousing roots and shoots of Romance grew
All through my mind and blood, and fruitful bore
　Harvests of ache and rapture, old and new,
Tumultuous serenity and more.

The sad and heavy fog of thwarted yearning
That looms in being seventeen and gay
　And Evangelical and ever turning
To vain and vague petitions I would pray
　For swift relief of my concupiscence
Gained sweet translucence as we drove away
　From dreary school to midday sustenance,

Contented in that muted ecstasy
  Of Bubba Sparxx's song "Deliverance,"
Nature's pomp, and his proximity.

  Tender intimacy unintimated
(Holy striving prevents my passion's stride),
  My heartbeat's rhythm unreciprocated
Across our natures' infinite divide—
  But while extremest hope's unrealized,
Denied desire is semi-satisfied
  By love that lacks in lust, a friendship prized
Like silver in gold's absence to console
  A youth that's otherwise demoralized
And wanting body warmth, has warmth of soul.

  I feasted on the grandest sandwich I'd
Ever in life consumed; receipt of joy
  Was also mine to see him smiling wide
In scatheless jesting (natural to a boy,
  Perpetual through manhood to a friend)
And in our laughter, only one annoy:
  That our convivial respite would end
Too quickly, severing the savor dear
  And so my teenage misery extend,
Freighting the burden of a single tear.

  Though hand and fingers pined for supple cheek
And craved the touch of close-cropped, frizzy hair
  I could, with some contentment, render meek
The longing, desperate longing for his fair
  Body and soul.—Out of this bane, a blessing,
A hearty belly-laugh to mock despair;
  Our happiness required no undressing!

And thus, across the gulf of eighteen years,
  Not for the dearth of amorous caressing
I sigh, but that we both can't share some beers.

SINGLE LIFE BLUES

Formless lover, realize!—
Satisfy my pining eyes
And be that concrete ecstasy
For arms now clutching vacancy.
All the transport and elation
I harvest in imagination
(Call it fancy, call it lust)
Is a diet but of dust.
I need substantial meals to feed
My hungry soul, my heart-sick need.
Take shape, my love, that you may be
Exiled from my fantasy,
Springing foreigner into
This kingdom of the real and true,
And my devotion naturalize
As citizen, my dream and prize.
You in the flesh, my longing quelled,
We shall in youthful raptures meld.

A warm and damp reality,
Struggling sensuality;
A private Eden we'd create,
Our twain appetites to sate.
Relaxed, perpetual embrace,
Eyes tethered to adoring face
(Wherefore into the soul to peer),
Whispers caress the tender ear
And breath upon the tingling neck,
As intrepid fingers trek

About the peaks and valleys of
The body of the one I love.
The chattering of wind-blown leaves
Filter, as they slip the eaves,
Through windows, beacons of the night:
Pearly lunar, stellar light.
And by this muted brilliance blessed
We'd drift into contented rest;
Our heartbeats synchronized in sleep
While angels silent vigils keep.

But for my pining, I can't find
You manifesting from my mind;
For all my aching passions roused,
My hermit-bed remains half-housed.
Half a soul inhabits me—
A gentle type of misery.

TO A CERTAIN KITTY

Creature of sweetest aristocracy
As lithe as wisps of smoke from candle-flame;
Lovely, gentle as moonlight on the sea;
Domestic, but too dignified to tame.

Snobby bitch, refusing the food I've bought you;
Destroyer of my couch—claws forged in Hell!
My home, reeking of your piss since I got you,
Is now your harried empire, held in thrall.

Thou little goddess of most tender love,
The sleek and living icon of all leisure;
Serenely playful emissary of
Profoundest prophecies of simple pleasure.

Selfish tyrant! Exigent for affection!
Unseen, deadly obstacle in my path!
Stubborn, impervious to all correction—
How can a thing so cute engender wrath?

A furry hum, companion to the lonely,
The marble-eyed posture of elegance;
So much devotion given me and only
Requiring the lowest maintenance.
    Darling! My love for you grows daily larger—
    Damnit, beast! Stop chewing on my phone charger!

PORTRAIT OF A CRISIS

The loneliness when you're lacking the love
  So ardently and boldly praised and promised,
And then you're scolded for ingratitude
                            For outstretched, empty hands;

This is the bitter savor of diminished
  Returns, heaping ladles of vacancy
Into a hungry bowl, disappointment
                            Being prohibited;

Disparity between the saints who find
  Their joy in agony, and I—too proud,
Too weak to cave into abandonment,
                            But writhing in a void;

It is the lovely sight of Ithaca,
  Scent of my homeland carried on the breeze—
Cruel Poseidon drags me an ocean thence
                            And hope is gouged from me.

AVIAN GOSPEL

Don't let this sparrow fall upon the ground
Lacking love in his heart. Convert the screeching
  Of bitterness into delightful sound,
A melody accordant with your teaching.
  Let me not lose my life with store and treasure,
Erecting barns to cram with hoarded gains.
  Let me be nourished only at your pleasure,
Secure to know your Providence sustains.
  You flood my life with torrents of correction,
Purging evil, confining me in refuge;
  Time passes, you release me to selection
Of branches and new home after deluge.
  You fashioned me on purpose with these wings;
  I seize the life and freedom that flight brings.

"ALL SORROWFUL AM I AND ALL TOO STOLID"

All sorrowful am I and all too stolid:
My soul is heavy with eternal winter—
Beneath the weight of weakness groans my solid
Self, more iron than flesh. Lord, let me splinter,

Crack and decay to atoms, or dissolve
My form into a pool of tears. Such need
Have I to weep and thus sore grieving solve—
Give me my cross to bear, but let me bleed.

SONNETS FOR KATHERINE

> "A faithful friend is a strong defense: and he that hath found him, hath found a treasure. Nothing can be compared to a faithful friend, and no weight of gold or silver is able to countervail the goodness of his fidelity."
> —Sirach 6:14–15

I.

The pale shadow of a summer night lifts
Its cloak, trickling illumination on
  An eager earth, while in the welkin drifts
A navy of clouds filigreed by dawn.
  Azure tones, golden light, a lukewarm breeze
Shiver a romance transporting and calm
  Commingled with fragrance of Mayday trees
That soothes the spirit with its airy balm.
  And yet this quietude of grandeur is
(For all its rush of fierce sublimity),
  But meager prelude to a greater bliss,
A joy that seems to touch infinity:
   I shall an afternoon and evening spend,
   Lost in felicity, with my best friend.

II.

    With suddenness to maim the gentle soul
In robbing the selfsame of sunlight's health,
    Despair attempts absconding, with the goal
Of wreaking poverty to summer's wealth.
    And as that sullen, cold bombardment drops
Its arsenal of moisture and of chill,
    The hope and cheer of friendship's union stops,
Captive to harbinger of frosty will.
    With inescapable prognostication,
I look months ahead to snow's drudgery—
    But sharp against the future's desolation,
A heat to counter winter's tyranny:
      A love indefinite, a loyal heart,
      Affection that can happiness restart.

III.

    So much did old Saint Valentine perceive
That in some centuries he'd have a rival,
    He did unto our Savior's bosom cleave
And beg for his own holy feast's survival.
    "Some intervention in her advent, pray,
For she'll engender so much love and ardor
    That I entreat You, Lord, her birth delay
Lest veneration flies your blessed martyr!"
    With sympathetic feeling for the saint
But larger pride in what He sought to fashion
    He reconciled the glory with complaint
And split the difference 'tween the twain to ration
      A full day's span from feast to Katherine's birth
      That's room enough for both their shining worth.

IV.

  Full seven sacraments our Lord ordained
To usher earthly souls to destined bliss,
  Infinitudes of surplus grace contained
In them, for heaven and for holiness.
  But in suffusing institution since
Our species' provenance, a sacrament
  Of nature hallows all from prole to prince
Which rescues human souls from detriment.
  A bath of shining love, a wholesome food
For personality, and secrets shared;
  A trove of memory confirmed for good
And kindred hearts and intellects are paired
  In sacred missions to eternity,
  Anointed by the balms of harmony.

V.

  Sinking, sinking with great celerity
Into the crushing fathoms of despair
  (Hamlet's bodkin solves Hamlet's quandáry),
Embracing death, my bed becomes my bier.
  The starry firmament of self-extinction
Emits some special radiance tonight,
  Self-hatred with omnipotent restinction
Snuffs self-esteem and hope's poor candlelight.
  A knock upon my door and unexpected,
Unbidden, but always welcome comes
  Angelic remedy to my dejected
Soul with salvific goal lest it succumb
  To the death-wish, of which she is the foe,
  And single-minded works to fight my woe.

VI.

  Reposed like Job, my hand upon my mouth,
And she with grace moves to Compassion's chair,
  Smiling a flood of pity on my drouth—
The lamp above illuminates her hair.
  A saint shall gain her halo after death
And vent grace, in glory, through centuries—
  But this current saint shines in drawing breath,
That breath dispelling all my miseries.
  The counterargument to suicide
Proclaims such restive confidence in me
  That the allure of Death I can't abide
Faced with such gentle objectivity.
  Let Thanatos harass with all his might,
  Soteria prevails in every fight.

AMAZING, SWEET

Moment of grace: exquisite extrication;
  Diversion from the path of my destruction;
The stepping-stone of divine filiation;
  A mangled soul now under reconstruction.
Torrent of grace: a capacious snowfall,
  Clothing the earth in freshest brilliancy.
Though soon, the mud and dirt that whiteness pall—
  Yet is, throughout the winter's tenancy,
Restored with new blanketings.—Action of grace:
  The self transported out of selfishness;
  New strength made manifest in helplessness;
The gradual unveiling of God's face;
  The sunshine of the universe upon
  Shrouded humanity; the battle won.

PRIORITIES

The pagan glory of grand Caesar's court,
Lost in its earthly pomp, received no news.
Parthia's Great King, deaf to the report
Of the momentous advent for the Jews

Stirred to nothing.—The local bigwigs slumbered
Uneasily for hazy prophecy,
Worried that Herod's days could well be numbered;
Murky omens, nameless anxiety.

And yet, for all the ignorance or dread
That slithered all around the crowns of earth,
No hail there was to Power, but instead
At the annunciation to the Birth

In humble fields where humbler shepherds dwelt
(The flung-off refuse of society),
A message where the stars in envy knelt
Before the glow of angel piety.

Those disregarded subjects of privation
Who labored to make other men more rich,
Observed the symphony of adoration,
Shared in that joy of superhuman pitch.

When awe had slackened slight, and they were able
(Bade by Heaven's emissaries to fly),
They sprinted full-speed to a certain stable
To where the infant Cosmic Prince did lie.

God knows His own priorities, is not
Impressed by the bejeweled rags of pride,
Regards worldly success as so much rot;
Let no one be confused as to the side

He blesses, represents, defends and favors;
Whose company that He prefers to share,
And that, for them, His Mercy never waivers
Nor Justice, for shirkers of their welfare.

METEOR CONFLICT

Weather: when Sky and Earth resume again
  Their ancient and dramatic lovers' quarrel—
Cloudy grimness; redundancy of rain;
  Hail's sting; blizzard's frigidity and whirl.
The Sky's rage is cold and brutal, but the Earth
  Has passion!—churning, caustic, hot and harsh:
Sylvan holocausts and volcanic wrath;
  The pungent, briny stench of beach and marsh.
  This is the climatology of spite
Which shutters a somber world to the Sun's rays
  And hides this world from that same solar sight;
The lovers' quarrel obscures the lovers' gaze.
  I cast these eyes of earth upward and sigh,
  Panting to catch again your eyes of sky.

KYRIE ELEISON

  the gory waterfall of calvary —
what else can cleanse the grime, the filthy sludge,
  the cuts and burns and bile make remedy
or else our species' wicked souls to budge?
  no romance was so gritty, nor a toil
for love so worth the name of agony,
  nor shame embraced that made the world recoil:
degradation redeems depravity
  the worldwide wail (that rattles heaven's walls)
of wretchedness that, knowing or denied,
  squeezes God's heart of mercy and recalls
why He in foul humiliation died
  and for that poignant and flamboyant death
  i kiss the crucifix with stinky breath

"I WAS THE LEAF YOU TROD UPON"

I was the leaf you trod upon
All shriveled on the autumn ground
That gave its crispy ghost up, and
Made that delicious crunchy sound.

I was the cigarette you lit
At break of day to clear your head;
The coffee, too—one burned, one boiled;
A sacrifice with prayers unsaid.

I was the beer you guzzled gayly
When you your birthday celebrated;
Imbibed but to massage your brain,
Consumed but to be urinated.

I was the lotion you employed
In your perverted solitude;
I'm now commingled with your seed
And down the drain, as gratitude.

We are the nation of the tools
And means of all your selfish pleasure:
The victims of your greed for fun,
Your delectation without measure.

Our corpses mark your decadence,
Your refuse is our cemetery:
Our silent dead are testament
To holocausts that keep you merry.

RENTBOY BLUES

The dim and orange glow of street-lamps drizzle
  Through curtain cracks, simulated fire-light;
Another fire that blazed begins to fizzle
                              And sputter in the night.

Relaxed, collapsed beneath a weight of bliss—
  The engines of Libido slow to rest—
I give my paramour a gentle kiss,
                              His head upon my breast.

It's like we are suspended in a snow
  Globe (flakes descending outside, after all);
A moment lovely, still—a peaceful show
                              Yet sole and mutual.

Transmitting all the tenderness and care
  That selfishness allows, I start to run
Sympathetic fingers through silken hair
                              And surely would have done

More, so much more for him—I would have made
  My home his, my goods his usufruct,
All my devotion offered had he stayed,
                              My independence chucked.

I loved him—love him still! So fair and gentle,
  A soul both meek and tough, docile mind and bright;
Humble reservoir of noble potential,
                              His wings unused for flight.

To meet his glances is to gulp the sea
  Of active hope between the desert isles
Of loneliness; and his proximity
                        His radiating smiles

Illuminate the dingy confine of
  My selfishness, and that to energize
Into the sweet activity of love—
                        Power of grins and eyes!

But fifty bucks, a pack of smokes, some weed
  Were trade enough for flesh's satisfaction;
And as for our hearts' coessential need—
                        'Twas canceled in transaction.

Whether God smiled or frowned, I cannot say;
  But we two broken boys in perfect pair
And perfect moment, in the darkness lay,
                        My fingers in his hair.

ST. THOMAS ON MISSION

  No time for airy phantoms of abstraction:
Faith is flesh and blood —it obliges motion
From hands and feet and lips to test devotion
  And atrophies when lacking name of action.
  My self was wrenched by this deliberate traction
Across cities, vast wastelands, and the ocean.
  And, though amazed by foreign tongues and faces
In trek and destination, still I see
Those Wounds which banished incredulity.
  The dead made living, breathing, talking, chases
  Away the shock of sundry tribes and races,
Reveals the image of divinity.
  Zeal smites me like a spear, and thus I wend
  The world, acquainting it with my best Friend.

FOR THE OLD MAN IN HIS TWILIGHT

The intellect will shrivel as the fragile body ages;
Encyclopedic minds can turn to volumes of blank pages.

For when I frolic through the fields of ever-blooming thought
To harvest rarest blossoms for delight of him who taught

Me first to sow and then to reap the flowers of ideas,
I've momentary happiness till I recall that he is

Now blind in eye and nose, and quite insensible to pleasure
He once received from these that he regarded as his treasure.

Their gaudy hues, their fragrances appeal to him no more
And I, in disenchantment drop the spray upon the floor.

Whatever joy in the bouquet I feel a mild despair:
Despite their loveliness, the flowers wilt which I can't share.

A POSTHUMOUS COMPETITION
-for Jesse Estrada

Honest Abe looked down from Heaven
    In curiosity
Upon his precious, blessed Union
    And bleakly sighed to see
The end result of all the progress
    Of our degeneracy.

"It's true," he candidly confessed,
    "That in my long-passed day
Chicanery and hate were norms—
    But still, I have to say
It's mighty steep that downward leap
    From Top Hat to Toupeé.

"My Grand Old Party has become
    A circus, it appears;
A carnival for bigotry
    And manufactured fears;
A priesthood of the currency
    Which it so reveres.

"And at its—and the country's—head:
    (What a frightful scene!)
A wind-up toy that seems designed
    To bully and demean,
A demagogic demi-god
    Of everything obscene!"

Old Andrew Jackson, down in Hell,
    Looked up at Paradise,
And sick of Lincoln's sulks, cried out,
    "Damn your sullen eyes!
It's plain to see my progeny
    Who lately lost the prize

"Are masters too, of greed and guile—
    But object to tasteless jokes!
Preferring heart-felt condescension
    To poor and swarthy folks;
That such, with eagerness and joy
    Might bear their oppressors' yokes.

"Talk the talk of Justice, and you
    Can walk the walk of Fraud;
And you can let your heart grow cold
    So long as your mind is broad;
Give your platitude an attitude
    And Twitter will applaud!

"It's a dubious horizon
    'Progressives' are marching toward,
When Lady MacBeth proving she's just
    As vicious as her lord
(And just as bumbling) means a point
    For Equality is scored."

Rail-Splitter and Ol' Hickory
    Thus argued back and forth
Which of the two respective parties
    Was of the lesser worth;
Whose descendant had brought the greater
    Scourge upon the earth?

By whom—Abe, or Andy's stock—
    Have the more lies been lied?
Whose heir, that with the larger store
    Of avarice and pride,
Has made the sanguine ocean of
    Mortality more wide?

Almighty God, overhearing
    This presidential fuss,
Looked down on the world, then at His watch—
    (Unpunctual, though just)—
Cracked His knuckles, and set to work
    To smite the earth to dust.

"FALSE ROMANCES SWARM ME LIKE LOCUSTS A FIELD"

False romances swarm me like locusts a field;
They blot out the sunlight of Goodness and Truth;
And rather than I to Reality yield
(And its comforts!), I pine for the riot of Youth.

The splendor and sickness of oats I was sowing
(The tally of venery setting my worth),
Or soaking my soul in the bowl that was flowing,
And my mind in the clouds of narcotical mirth.

Or else, I might stupidly mourn the delay
Of virginity's loss, or my drab adolescence;
As if joyous and sensual brilliance of day
Should shine through all things in a happy quintessence.

I thirst for a desert and pine for a corpse;
I regret any virtue and spurn its reward;
How deftly nostalgia for wickedness warps
The resolve of a spoiled little brat of the Lord.

But then the diminished returns I recall
And the hungry compulsions that never were sated—
The ladder of sand I ascended, though tall,
Upon the first rung my endeavors negated.

Though the harems of Arcady lusciously teem
With the promise of harvest at happiness' summit,
It is but a rosy, inimical dream
Of soaring desires and fruitions that plummet.

The painful frustration of so many years
Eventually led me to wisdom, and choose
To smash pleasure's idols, be baptized by tears,
Lest every fulfillment in life I should lose.

Now ardor and joy are not strangers to me,
But I find that they glitter far less than I thought;
Though silver and gold better ornaments be
They lack the endurance of iron when wrought.

Maturity beckons as Memory sighs,
The song of the sirens by angels is mute;
The flower delectable shrivels and dies
To engender the nourishing sweetness of fruit.

"AIN'T EASY TO BE CATHOLIC AND GAY"

Ain't easy to be Catholic and gay—
  Disused libido wreaks a fierce frustration;
What can a sinner like me do but pray?

It seems that all throughout and every day
  I must perform a spiritual castration;
Ain't easy to be Catholic and gay.

I have no means this passion to allay
  (The eye of God is privacy's privation):
What can a sinner like me do but pray?

I have a rising river of dismay
  At such a superhuman expectation.
Ain't easy to be Catholic and gay.

I have not fluent pen enough to say
  And justice do to this my desolation;
What can a sinner like me do but pray?

And finally, if I should go astray,
  I would be playing chicken with damnation!
Ain't easy to be Catholic and gay—
What can a sinner like me do but pray?

THE RAVEN'S SOLILOQUY

Let the eagle be haughty and soar through his zone;
Let the robin and chickadee chirp melody;
Let the goose be boastful of where he has flown;
Let the seagull erupt in cacophonous glee—

But I am the glory of mischief and mirth
Possessed of a mettle and intellect rare,
The eloquent sentinel-jester of earth,
The acrobat-goddess unconquered in air.

I am clothed in the midnight bereft of the moon
And the stars with their storied and twinkling light;
An autonomous shadow a-wing in the noon
And the rustle of silk is the sound of my flight.

I sip from the goblet of cunning to feed
On the affluent feast which you recklessly waste.
I spend but a shred to supply all my need
And gorge on the scraps of your decadent race.

But those of your kind that deliberately serve
To supply me a sustenance, freely I seek
Some trinkets of gratitude that they deserve
And receive by the grace of my mind and my beak.

Some tribes of your species give credence that I
Gave form from the mud by the Maker's decree
Your bodies; your souls, these I plucked from the sky—
The stars!—and installed them fastidiously.

But your greed and your pride were all your own making:
The surplus of earth you did surfeit upon.
You regarded all Nature as yours for the taking—
Entitlements based on your brain and your brawn.

This hubris compelled me to fashion the bear
And the walrus to slay you in arrogant error;
So that in your vice, should you fail to beware,
These teachers shall teach through mortality's terror.

Am I your custodian, witness, or friend?
The myth and the mystery's yours to decide;
As you ponder and gape on the earth, I ascend
To clasp with the welkin and chant as I glide.

"MY LIFE IS CONSTANT AUTUMN"

My life is constant autumn, and the summer
Eludes me, hides in far exotic climes.
I hear of its festivity, and glummer
Grow and begin to think existence rhymes

With everything that floats in melancholy;
The flotsam of my youthful aspirations.
And all that is romantic, bright, and jolly—
Well, that's reserved for other folks' vacations.

The fragrant tones of verdure do not greet
Me at the daybreak, nor a floral scent;
My skin is uncaressed by sunshine's heat,
My pensive soul unstirred by merriment.

Effete rain falling from a pallid sky
Arouses the desire to hibernate;
Experience itself is one long sigh
Of languid chills that gloom and enervate.

Yet, there are days when clouds are scrubbed away,
Revealing all the sapphire majesty
Above, and heaven's solar crown, whose ray
Illumes with highest pitch of clarity

The earth beginning to recline and snooze
Beneath the drooping emeralds turned to gold,
Which drop to golden blanket, and suffuse
All their brilliance o'er the heady mould.

In lukewarm light and in the lively breeze
I sense the strum of a supernal harp;
I shed my sadness and then stroll with ease
To unheard music both sedate and sharp.

To eastward, mountains—those gigantic idols
Of human wish for distant vistas—bruise
In splendor as the vibrant crimson sidles
Up their grand slopes, like blushes of a Muse.

Incipience of frost in evening air,
Commingled with the silver starlight shining:
These added to the aforementioned fair
Repose the tear and put a pause on pining.

While lacking passion of the year's high noon,
I have a tamer, ripened joy instead:
As different as the bliss of honeymoon
From when a couple's fifty autumns wed.

EUROPE IS THE LESS

(to the tune of "Lorena")

-for Cameron and Tiffany

As sunset's winking out, my darling,
I call to share tomorrow's dawn
And snatch that fleeting ray, my darling,
To soothe when your own sunshine's gone.
As callous space and time defy
Our love, with all the scorn of fate;
We sigh beneath the selfsame sky,
Though half the planet separate.

Three months deprived of you, companion,
A further three till my return.
Of home and love by work, companion,
I'm robbed and left to ache and yearn.
I pine for native mountains, town,
The climate, flora, fauna, food—
For more than these, in tears I drown,
When thoughts of you my mind intrude.

My thoughts all captive to you, lover,
Though fair distractions gird me round.
They're nothing to your beauty, lover,
All drabness is this foreign ground.
Yes, all the pomp of Europe fades;
Banal its ancient charms and grace.
Its grandeur into dust degrades
When I recall my lover's face.

But let despair be hushed, my sweetheart,
Though pain of absence soaks the eye;
Though time and space now part us, sweetheart,
Those selfsame soon our tears will dry.
A season hence I'll step the earth,
And reunited with my queen
In raptures of romantic mirth,
We'll bid adieu to partings keen.

FOR TANNER

   A walking, breathing shrine of timeless Youth,
Of wisdom wove through gay philosophy;
   And all that's blithe and glamorous in Truth
Is grace for those who share his company.
   A heart to thaw the harshest winter's snow,
A vibrant jolt to shake mundanity,
   A personality of golden glow
Outshining base and brass humanity.
   His features, let's say… Adonis to the life!
And thus, objectively, the civil war
   Within himself ain't worth the cruel strife
Waged ruthlessly against his self-rapport.
   Would that I could to him affection lend
   He'd see him as I rightly see my friend.

THE LAST POEM

Long epochs hence our present age
In strange, remote futurity,
The Genius of the human race
Will then exceed maturity

And slide into a senile fog,
And then extremis, and then death.
For that unknown but certain day
The Muses wait with bated breath.

Exhausted will the ancient mines
Of Creativity then be,
As will the fertile soil of Tropes
And all Originality.

Invincible Ennui will bleed
And banalize Experience,
And every human culture will
Be damned in Final Decadence.

And lo, the Twilight of the Arts
Is consummate, or nearly there:
A poet, with a pen in hand, is
Seated at Inspiration's chair,

And scribbles out some decent verse
Extracted from his own heart's quarry,
A polished literary gem
About—fitting!—the sunset's glory.

The geriatric Muses nine
Release a last and gentle sigh
Of sweet relief, and peacefully
Suffer aneurysm, and then die.

The critics, with rapacious force—
Imperious community!—
And anxious of their livelihood,
Arise in wrathful unity

To seize upon the final word
And shred to bits the poet's ode;
God intervenes, and mercifully,
He makes the setting sun explode.

"IMPOTENCE RAVES AT A DEAF UNIVERSE"

Impotence raves at a deaf universe:
Articulated static fragmentating
 A mind, capacities already worse
For waste, and for abuse exacerbating
 The want and weakness that at first compelled
The soul to make his flight from all the danger
 And disappointment faced in life. Enshelled
In enervation and escape, a stranger
 To Reason now, as well as avatar
Of stark inadequacy, and recalling
 Each injury that left a jagged scar
And every vicious insult and appalling.
 Resentment, all humiliation feeling,
 Bereft of justice, recompense, and healing.

THE CAUTIONARY TALE OF PUGNACIOUS PETER

Pugnacious Peter loved to bellow
  And babble out a strange refrain:
"Zero fucks given!" the silly fellow
  Would bawl and belch again and again
With constant ostentation, as if he
Deserved a medal for his apathy.

Like the howls of philandering cats,
  Or a full-flow urinal's flushing;
Like a forest of animal scats,
  Or the pus of a pimple gushing;
Such was the impression felt and made
By his selfish, douchey gasconade.

Deaf to facts which he labeled "excuses";
  Stone to the touch of another's feelings;
Blind in the sight that Pity produces;
  Anxious to frame his own low ceilings
Of charity and tolerance,
This patron saint of Indifference.

Poor Peter's proud pugnacity
  Gave tongue to his unsought views
Which he slammed with harsh tenacity
  Into the ears of those who'd refuse
Their hasty, unconditional assent
To opinions he aired without their consent.

With a bully's zeal, he spared no pain
  Or expense at another's distress
In single pursuit of his own gain
  And comfort and ruthless success.
Ambitious, haughty and high-maintenance:
The ass-clownish apex of exigence.

Alas! such tawdry temerity
  And rejection of solidarity
For his Gospel of Severity...
  Estranged him from Reality!
Employed in egotistical vocation
He never expected its reciprocation.

For Peter—who did not give a fuck
  And was so supremely proud of it—
Was often with amazement struck
  When others did not give a shit
What he thought, felt, wished, needed or believed;
Zero fucks he gave, zero he received.

And every trouble and every doubt
  To which our mortal flesh is heir
Peter must face and bear without
  The comfort of another's care,
Nor other's joy, acclaim, and pride to bless
The hallmarks and rewards of his success.

Peter's fortunes soon petered out;
  Now the whirlwind's harvest he reaps,
And silently, this wretched lout
  (An island entire of self) weeps.
And reflecting upon his own bad luck,
Repents: "God! I wish I'd given a fuck!"

MORAL

The moral is, I scarcely need spell out,
That those too quick and eager to yell out
And boast of their own lack of fucks to give
Will have an absolutely sordid life to live.

DOGGEREL BY A HOMEBODY

I rise from sleep, I take a shower,
I brush my teeth, I shave my face,
I don my clothes, invent a smile,
To satisfy the human race.

Sometimes they like me, sometimes they don't;
Manners and wit yield mixed results.
I comprehend but clumsily
Propriety between adults.

The guessing games, the gossip mills,
The feuds, the cliques, the power plays,
The awkward blush, the pang of doubt,
The fear of scorn, the thirst for praise;

Here, egos spar in silly strife;
There, egos pair in dubious dance;
My own's got scars and blistered feet
From years of social circumstance,

With shit to show for it, it seems,
But a tendency to brood and fret;
And a fortune from that dual-largesse
Of Time: Resentment and Regret.

Sick of shyness and self-promotion,
Ashamed of my own ineptitude;
Daily drained by others "drama;"—
I elect a life of Solitude.

Alone!—and to live by no one's leave,
And to enjoy the quiet mind
And the cozy satisfaction that
In the outside world, I cannot find.

Alone!—to thaw the bitter frost
Of outworn or neglected Love;
To lick the wounds of disappointment,
To cease to pine, to cease to loathe.

I play my music, or on my Xbox,
I binge-watch Netflix until dawn,
I read one hundred pages daily,
'Cuz the human race makes me yawn.

I puff a joint, I smoke a cig,
I slam a shot, I rub one out,
I relish sleep, I wait for Death,
'Cuz the human race has worn me out.

DOGGEREL ON BEATITUDE

Happy the man who builds a pyre
  And, lacking for a ram,
Shall whet his hungry knife and weep
  The tears of Abraham.

Happy the woman who ascends
  Breathlessly, in travail
(Blinded by sweat, parched for a drink),
  The steep and narrow trail.

Happy the eunuch (for the sake
  Of heaven's kingdom gaining)
Who banishes his nature to
  The desert of abstaining.

Happy the dogged supplicant
  Who at the gate is knocking,
In need of bread, who will not cease
  Until the door's unlocking.

Happy the martyr the hangman burns
  Or crucifies or flays,
Who 'midst the blood and agony
  Has on his lips God's praise.

Happy are those enduring scorn
  Or dearth or lowliness;
All these are blessed —but tell me, please:
  What is unhappiness?

"WHAT IS IT 'BOUT A SUMMER NIGHT"

What is it 'bout a summer night
That conjures blood into a yearning?
Is it the ghost of Paradise
That stirs up such unquiet churning?

A dreamy haze of lemonade
About the mountains charms the eye,
Transmuted soon to grander tones—
The roseate and eastern sky;

And 'gainst the watercolors, boldly
Tower the birch and cottonwood
And all their leafy silhouettes
In light and shadow's brotherhood.

The sunshine's slumber wakens cool
And soothing exhalations sweet
To calm the soul and body in
Relief from the aestival heat.

And I, all sighs and throbbing heart,
With gleaming, poignant visions haunting
My troubled spirit; past and future
Frolics and adventure wanting.

The goals of these Edenic raptures
Some time ago I piled a pyre.
More solemn now, but still I long
To chew the apple of desire,

And would have better luck in struggle
With passion in my solitudes:
But miserly of brilliant stars
Are skies in northern latitudes

This season, and their consolations;
I think my heart would be less riven
Could I in summer's pleasures bask
Beneath the audience of heaven.

WHO WOULD FARDELS BEAR?
-for Jared Snively

  The bottom of the ocean ain't so dark
Nor crushing as the slow fatality
  Of hope, a misery so damned and stark
You pine to expedite mortality.
  I am within a gloomy maze without
An entrance or an exit, save the stream
  Of blood I would erupt from wrists that shout
For sharp release, and then the vacant dream
  Of ultimate nonentity. My life
Is conscious death, a singularity
  Of pain; wherefore endure?—when this sweet knife
Can usher me into tranquility
  Never to loathe, writhe, dread, despair or crave,
  But slumber infinite within a grave.

THE POMEGRANATE TREE
for Paul and Rachel Curran

Weary, thirsty, in a new land, I sought
For nature's craving, rest and sustenance.
So far, my parching pilgrimage had brought
Little respite from grueling Providence.

Trudging infinite uphill, a false peak—
The sad result of all my facile hope—
Displays ordeals of vistas that my weak
Breathing corpse, shrill with aching, could not cope

With.—Soon however, heart gladdened, I see
With welcome boughs laden with fruit and shade
A large, double-trunked Ebenezer tree
Which, sighting it, despair began to fade.

Abundant leisure; succulence to eat;
Fragrance teeming like skyward-rising prayers;
Enclave of coolness in oppressive heat;
A cemetery to inter my cares.

Ubiquity of rocks and dust defined
The wasteland of my sojourn's drudgery:
But a slight, verdant paradise I find
For me about the pomegranate tree.

BETWEEN INSANITY AND DOUBT

When even placid days are fraught
  With all the fire of mental hell
That smolders now, then blazes hot,
  And suffocates me in my cell—
Ponder the uselessness of thought.

The true and noble, pure and fine
  That Mind discovers and then hallows
So that the Will might then align—
  My cancerous cognition swallows
These, birthing tumors fat, malign.

The function fades and madness swells
  To overcrowd the understanding;
A metastasis that impels
  Surrender to Despair's demanding,
And meager Hope's resistance quells.

Between insanity and doubt
  (The haziness of truth and fraud),
One manifold, incessant shout
  Rings out and drowns the voice of God,
Obscures the eudaemonic route.

A pall, an artificial night
  Is cast upon my days and dreams;
Confusion, rage distract my sight—
  But still, through all this blockage beams
A small, but constant shaft of light.

SELF-REBUKE

it can be difficult to buck up
when you're convinced that you're a fuck-up
your friends may tell you otherwise
try to believe their honest lies

allay the dearth of hope with pleasure
the nervous system's buried treasure
that bullion to coinage shape
by which you purchase your escape

but saturnine reality
casts a pall on levity
night envelops joys diurnal
life is short and hell's eternal

since the pursuit of merriment
will rarely ever make a dent
in the iron gauze that parts
the joy we crave and our sad hearts

perhaps the moody melancholic
instead of finding ways to frolic
might bear the crucifixion labor
and try to serve his god and neighbor

for love—not pleasing fancy's bliss—
and its attendant sacrifice
and some degree of self-control
make happy the unhappy soul

THE SEARCH FOR EUTERPE

I searched for her among the grass and flowers;
Within a fecund forest and a glade;
Beside a limpid creek, 'neath vernal bowers
Which the weary perambulator shade.

I scanned for her among the starry heaven
Awash in great ribbony luminescence:
A grand and rapturous celestial sweven
That'd make an atheist to feel God's presence.

I sought for her in friendship's bonds and treats—
Say, conviviality around a fire;
And in the heat and joy between the sheets,
Lovers' embraces, or when loves expire.

I looked in sacred texts and liturgies
And deep within spirituality—
I'd find her momentarily in these,
And spying me, she'd flip me off and flee.

"I WOULD HAVE HANDLED THEM WITH GREATER CARE"

I would have handled them with greater care
Had someone told me just how deadly dreams
  Can be—these Petri dishes of despair,
Failure flourishing from what fortune seems.
  Some dreams, too large, you swallow and then choke;
Some dreams, poisonous, as they're gaudy-hued;
  Some dreams, unrealized, weigh like a yoke;
Some dreams brighten, the more they you elude.
  But to defer (and not indulge) will cause
Them not to shrivel, but metastasize
  And eat your life away, without a pause.—
Bethink, whether you seek or shirk your prize:
  Our joys have no census; we only count
  Our tears, and further weep at the amount.

ASTRONOMICAL DOGGEREL

stars puncture sight
and thus usurp the night
rebel against the void to show
some glory to poor souls below
the clouds and darkness fail
to spread a veil

that can obscure
for long their brightness pure
the steady stream of ancient light
that for its trek retains a bright
prophetic beam of hope
by which we cope

with all the piss
of pique and loneliness
these glad effusions of creation
unhindered sprint the desolation
of interstellar spaces
to touch our faces

which—if we're willing—
give action to instilling
resolve to greater confidence
reflecting stellar radiance
expand internal leaven
by heat of heaven

"OBSCURED AZURE: THE HEAVENS' AIRY FOUNTAINS"

  Obscured azure: the heavens' airy fountains
Send sprinklings of cold kisses from the sky;
  Or like monstrous ghosts, curl about the mountains,
Haunting the vales beneath to satisfy
  The thirsty earth, which drinks its greedy fill
To surfeit, and releases from the bond
  Of potency (by every plucky rill)
The act of seed and flower, stalk and frond.
  It's natural that the human race complains
Of veils upon the sunshine's levity;
  But still, the heavy torrent of the rain's
Coequal to the sun's vitality.
  Both aqueous bombardment, solar beam
    Combined in cycle make the earth to teem.

"RECIPIENT OF MUSTARD SEED"

Recipient of mustard seed
  And told to move Denali,
I gaped in mute perplexity
  In that unhaunted valley,

As lonely as a teardrop shed
  Upon a desert dune,
Compelled to irrigate a waste
  As barren as the moon.

Was it a promise or a warning?
  Is it hope or is it threat?
Does He command what can't be done,
  Or is He just all wet?

Such is an expectation that
  Can make you weep a fountain,
When you can't find a precedent
  Of one that moved a mountain.

CONVERSION II

   Rogue world, alone, adrift upon the void,
Eternal bedfellow to cosmic dust;
   Contented to all stellar realms avoid,
Basking in placid darkness; and my crust
   Rimed o'er in stillborn atmosphere and seas—
A global frost as hard as adamant!
   No eye beholds my vast topographies,
No neighbor treks across my firmament.
   Yet nudged a bit by universal motions,
     A star arrests me with its phantom forces
     And dreaded sunlight floods upon my face:
Now slowly ice melts into sky and oceans,
   Zoetic flourishings shall run their courses,
   And I have found community in space.

DOGGEREL BY AN IRRESOLUTE FELLOW

Inconstancy, thy name is Michael;
Begin afresh the endless cycle.
New notions and emotions trickle,
Move from faithful back to fickle.
Firm and pious resolution
Soon dissolves to dissolution;
Then misery of wantonness
Converts to pain of soberness.
A soaring romance goes to war
Against a passion's mighty roar.
They duke it out, round for round,
Upon myself, the battleground.
And neither side is winning, losing—
It falls on me, the weight of choosing.
I make this, then that decision;
I make a jump-rope of volition.
"And this, too, shall pass away,"
To return another day.

DECLINE AND FALL

Doom of the summer particulate, falling;
  The cold, a sleeping goddess, wakes
In premature intensity, and shawling
  The flirty earth with pallid flakes
      Of nunnish modesty,
      Sudden sobriety,
  Creates a ghostly landscape sprawling
As Life, her silent sacrament, partakes.

The roiling, fresh ecumenopolis
  Of blood and sap and bloom and breath
Was unprepared for the untimely kiss
  Of glittering and frigid death.
      Romps of fertility
      Freeze in sterility;
  The grand zoetic edifice
Is mummified beneath the frosty sheath.

It is the twilit widowhood of Nature;
  Her shrouded face, a solid shower
Of pearl and silver, warning every creature:
  "You know not what the day or hour!"
      Now all the human race is
      Collapsed into a stasis
  Of selfish enmity's procedure,
Forsaking loving warmth for chill of power.

BALLAD OF MADNESS

When gears are ground and bolts come loose,
  And all the coils unwind
And sunshine's splendor fades into
  The midnight of the mind:

The vultures of insanity
  Descend upon their prey—
The carrion of intellect;
  The soul that rots away.

The contents found in Reason's tomb
  Are hard to excavate,
And harder still to reassemble
  And to resuscitate.

Hallucination is your comrade;
  Your bedfellow, Delusion.
Anxiety, your lifelong guide,
  Companioned by Confusion.

A constant stupor, as if in
  A fog that follows you;
A cloud of incoherence that
  Almost swallows you.

The host of fears that slowly make
  You victim to their maw:
A multitude of ants assailing
  Your scrumptious flesh to gnaw.

You swallow fourteen pills a day;
  Twelve hours in your bed
For daily sleep—all to sedate
  The monster in your head.

It's not that friends and counselors
  Don't help—of course they do!—
The Dutch boy's finger in the dam
  Stops water coming through.

The flood, however, bursts upon
  The village down below;
The hapless villagers themselves
  Must fend against the flow.

Thus while I have a universe
  Of glowing gratitude
For loved ones' love—my plight remains
  One of solitude.

And though I hope for Heaven's joy
  Someday—a second birth—
I must endure, this little while,
  A tiny Hell on earth.

"EXOTICAL NEUROLOGY"

Exotical neurology
Creates a thirst for the mundane;
   Give me the tedium of sanity!

   Consider what may seem inanity:
My soul, the tenant of defective brain,
 At its eviction, flies to Judgment Seat
   (Here madness meets theology),
 And there Creator meet;
How would I recognize Him in His glory?
  Perhaps hallucinating evil,
  I think that he's the devil?

  Suppose I pass the test;
   Before I enter rest,
He has me do a stint in Purgatory.
 I may mistake that fire
   That purifies
 For that of sulfurous damnation
 And, in despairing, lose salvation
(Tremendous irony and dire!).

  But should I rise,
 And in ascending to eternal bliss
I might succumb to paranoia, doubting
My happy residence, and shouting
    "Conspiracy, conspiracy!"
   At saints and angels for eternity.
 Some folks may scoff at this

And wonder if I understand
   What's meant by "Paradise."
  But they have not had to endure
   What I have had to, twice:
    Reality's unraveling,
    An earthquake leveling
The city of the mind, and then withstand
 A life of aftershocks, and cope
  Without a cure.

One takes for granted the coherence
Of actuality, and trusts appearance;
 But let such shatter into shards
   And then be reassembled clumsily—
 One might let wither any hope
Of an eventual illumination.
   My only hope is God allowing me,
If I am saved, to bring my medication
  And dwell in Heaven's psychiatric wards.

REASON IN THE FACE OF MADNESS

If I again the ancient faith renounced
  For fairer modern creeds of skepticism;
From all romance with superstition flounced
  Away, into the bed of humanism—
Shook shackles off by ratiocination,
  Followed the breadcrumbs of enlightenment,
And hotly chased the scent of liberation,
  Nurtured belligerence of temperament,
And drank godlessness unto my fill,
                        My mind would still be ill.

If I could nail myself to twenty crosses
  Or bear them up the rocky, narrow trail,
Regarding worldly gains as empty losses
  And breathlessly pursuing without fail
Holiness, as the eagle hunts her quarry;
  Gave all my property to poverty,
Myself to flames, all for His kingdom's glory,
  And mastered chastity and charity,
Shone with temperance and nevermore was lazy
                        I still would be quite crazy.

If I with keenest eyes of wisdom could
  Untangle all the knots of mystery;
If all that could be known, I understood,
  And mastered science and philosophy—
If biases I could dissolve and squarely
  Look in the face of objectivity;
Presumed to deal with all God's children fairly

And shouldered all of logic's gravity:
Could I of intellect all powers gain
                            I would remain insane.

INCREMENTAL IMMUTABILITY

Up from the fathoms of the self
Rose the desire, and surfacing
Into the sunlight of volition,
Became a continent of action.

mark the moment of consummation
subtle as phases of the moon
as indecipherable as noon
foggy, murky as speciation

Cliffs soared, eroded into beaches;
Mountains towered, then stooped to valleys;
Forests flourished, then by axe or fire
Consumed; but still the land endured.

between the candle and the comet
between the whisper and the storm
between the cradle and the worm
between the whiskey and the vomit

Upthrusting into being—yet
Though ever changing, cannot wear
Away or easily erase
Geology of character.

infinitude of slight gradations
that run from choice to consequence
in good or in malevolence
unseen in prior speculations

So, stamped for eons on the world,
The glaring bedrock that we form
Exposed and inescapable,
Unchanged until eternity.

WRITER'S BLOCK

Impotence on one's wedding night;
A guitarist with broken fingers;
A single beer left in the fridge;
Laryngitical chamber singers.

Construction barring a road trip;
A lost appetite at a feast;
A longing for verdure in winter;
A parish deprived of a priest.

These sorrows I've listed could serve
As semblance to the writer's curse—
Scratch that; now that I ponder it,
They don't come close; the block is worse.

www.ingramcontent.com/pod-product-compliance
Lightning Source LLC
Chambersburg PA
CBHW061454040426
42450CB00007B/1351